TRENDS & STRATEGIES IN THE STOCK MARKET BULL RUN

TUSHAR RAJ

Made with ♥ on the Notion Press Platform
www.notionpress.com

To all the investors and traders who have taken the time to dive into the world of stock market, this book is dedicated to you.

Without your curiosity and your willingness to take risks, the stock market would not be the exciting and dynamic environment that it is today. You are the ones who keep the markets alive, and who drive innovation and growth in the global economy.

We also want to extend a special thanks to the countless experts and analysts who have shared their insights and knowledge with us throughout the years. Your research and experience have been invaluable in shaping the strategies and trends that we explore in this book.

Last but not least, we dedicate this book to our families and loved ones who have supported us through thick and thin. Your unwavering love and encouragement have made it possible for us to pursue our passion for the stock market and share our insights with the world.

Thank you all for being a part of this journey, and we hope that the insights and strategies shared in this book will help you achieve your investment goals and navigate the exciting world of stock market with confidence and success.

Sincerely,

Tushar Raj

Contents

Foreword

Welcome to "Trends & Strategies in the Stock Market Bull Run," a comprehensive guide to navigating the current state of the stock market. In recent years, the stock market has experienced a historic bull run, and it's more important than ever for investors to stay informed and strategic when making investment decisions.

This guide is designed to help investors of all levels understand the latest trends and strategies for success in the stock market. Whether you're a seasoned investor or just starting out, this guide will provide you with valuable insights and information to make informed decisions and achieve your investment goals.

In the first section of this guide, we'll take a closer look at the current state of the stock market, including its recent performance and the factors that are driving this historic bull run. We'll explore the latest trends and patterns in the market, and discuss how investors can take advantage of these trends to make smart investment decisions.

In the second section, we'll dive into some of the key strategies that investors can use to navigate the stock market bull run. We'll discuss the importance of diversification, risk management, and investment discipline, and provide practical tips for implementing these strategies in your own investment portfolio.

Throughout the guide, we'll also feature insights and perspectives from leading experts in the field of investment and finance. These experts will share their own experiences and expertise, providing valuable advice and guidance to help investors make the most of this exciting time in the stock market.

At the end of the guide, we'll provide a summary of the key takeaways and actionable steps that investors can take to optimize their investment strategy in the current bull run. We hope that this guide will serve as a valuable resource for investors looking to stay informed, strategic, and successful in the stock market.

Thank you for joining us on this journey, and we wish you all the best in your investment endeavors.

Sincerely,
Tushar Raj

Preface

Dear Reader,

Welcome to "Trends & Strategies in the Stock Market Bull Run." In this book, we explore the latest trends and strategies in the stock market that have been instrumental in the current bull run. The stock market is a dynamic and constantly evolving landscape, and keeping up with the latest trends and strategies can be a daunting task. That's why we've created this book to provide you with the insights you need to navigate this ever-changing environment.

The last few years have been particularly remarkable for the stock market, with many investors seeing significant gains. This bull run has been fueled by a range of factors, including low-interest rates, government stimulus packages, and the rapid adoption of technology. These factors have created a perfect storm for investors, making the stock market an attractive option for those seeking to grow their wealth.

However, while the stock market can be a lucrative investment opportunity, it's not without its risks. That's why it's essential to have a deep understanding of the latest trends and strategies in the market. In this book, we cover a range of topics, including the impact of technology on the stock market, the rise of ESG investing, and the importance of diversification.

Whether you're a seasoned investor or just starting, this book has something for you. Our aim is to provide you with the knowledge and tools you need to make informed investment decisions and succeed in the current bull run.

We hope you find this book informative and engaging. Thank you for choosing "Trends & Strategies in the Stock Market Bull Run."

Best regards,

Tushar Raj

Acknowledgements

I would like to express my deepest gratitude to all the individuals who have contributed to the creation and publication of this book, "Trends & Strategies in the Stock Market Bull Run". Without their help, guidance, and support, this book would not have been possible.

First and foremost, I would like to thank my editor, Kishan Rai, for their insightful feedback and guidance throughout the writing process. Their expertise and attention to detail have been invaluable in shaping this book into its final form.

I would also like to express my gratitude to the reviewers who provided feedback on early drafts of the book. Their thoughtful comments and suggestions helped to improve the clarity and quality of the content.

I am deeply indebted to the research team that contributed to this book. Their tireless efforts in gathering and analyzing data, as well as their expertise in the field, have greatly enriched the book's content.

I would like to extend my appreciation to the designers and layout artists who worked on the book's layout and design. Their creativity and attention to detail have resulted in a visually stunning and engaging book.

Lastly, I would like to thank my friends and family for their unwavering support and encouragement throughout the writing process. Their love and belief in me have been my constant source of inspiration and motivation.

Thank you to all those who contributed to this book. I am honored to have worked with such a talented and dedicated team, and I hope that this book will provide readers with valuable insights into the exciting world of stock market trends and strategies.

Prologue

Welcome to "Trends & Strategies in the Stock Market Bull Run." As the name suggests, this book is all about the latest trends and strategies that are shaping the stock market and how you can take advantage of them.

The stock market is a complex and dynamic place, and it can be difficult to navigate if you don't have the right information and tools. That's where this book comes in. Our goal is to provide you with the knowledge and insights you need to make informed decisions and succeed in the stock market.

Whether you're a seasoned investor or just starting out, this book will help you stay ahead of the curve and capitalize on the latest opportunities. We'll cover everything from the hottest stocks and sectors to watch, to the latest tools and techniques for analyzing the market and making informed decisions.

But we don't just focus on the trends - we also provide practical, actionable strategies for making the most of them. We'll show you how to build a diversified portfolio, manage risk, and develop a long-term investment strategy that can help you achieve your financial goals.

Of course, the stock market can be unpredictable, and no one can guarantee success. But with the right knowledge and strategies, you can increase your chances of success and make the most of the opportunities that come your way.

So, whether you're a seasoned investor or just starting out, we invite you to join us on this journey through the latest trends and strategies in the stock market bull run. Let's get started!

Author Info

Tushar Raj

ONE

Welcome to "Trends & Strategies in the Stock Market Bull Run." In this chapter, we'll introduce you to the concept of the stock market bull run, what it means, and why it matters.

Simply put, a bull market is a period of time when stock prices are rising, and investor sentiment is generally positive. A bull run is a prolonged period of bullish market activity, which can last for months or even years. During a bull run, many investors are optimistic about the future, and they are willing to take on more risk in pursuit of higher returns.

There are several factors that can contribute to a bull run, including economic growth, low interest rates, and positive news about individual companies or sectors. Bull runs can be exciting and profitable, but they can also be risky, as investor sentiment can quickly shift if the market experiences a downturn.

So why does the stock market bull run matter? For one, it can be a good opportunity for investors to make money. Stocks tend to perform well during bull runs, and many investors see significant gains during these periods.

But there are also broader economic implications to consider. A bull run can be a sign of a healthy economy, with growing businesses, rising employment, and strong consumer confidence. On the other hand, a prolonged bull run can also lead to overconfidence and risky behavior, which can ultimately lead to a market correction or even a crash.

In this book, we'll explore the latest trends and strategies in the stock market bull run, and show you how to make informed investment decisions to maximize your returns and manage your risk. Whether you're a seasoned investor or just starting out, this book will provide you with the tools and knowledge you need to navigate this exciting and dynamic market.

So let's get started!

TWO

In this chapter, we'll explore the concept of market cycles and trends and how they can impact your investments. Understanding these patterns is essential to making informed decisions in the stock market bull run.

1. Market Cycles

First, let's define what we mean by a market cycle. A market cycle refers to the regular pattern of ups and downs in the stock market over time. These cycles can last anywhere from a few months to several years.

Market cycles typically have four stages: accumulation, markup, distribution, and markdown. During the accumulation phase, investors start to buy stocks as they become undervalued. In the markup phase, stocks start to rise as more investors get on board. In the distribution phase, investors start to sell off their holdings, leading to a decline in the market. Finally, in the markdown phase, stocks hit bottom and investors start to accumulate again.

2. Trends

Trends are longer-term patterns in the market that can last for several years. There are three types of trends: uptrends, downtrends, and sideways trends. An uptrend is characterized by higher highs and higher lows, while a downtrend has lower highs and lower lows. A sideways trend, also known as a range-bound market, is where prices move within a relatively narrow range.

3. Identifying Trends and Cycles

Now that we've defined market cycles and trends, let's talk about how to identify them. One way to do this is by using technical analysis. Technical analysis involves studying charts and other market data to identify patterns and trends.

Another way to identify trends and cycles is by using fundamental analysis. Fundamental analysis involves looking at a company's financial and economic data, such as earnings reports and economic indicators, to make investment decisions.

4. Investing in Market Cycles and Trends

Once you've identified the current market cycle and trend, you can make more informed investment decisions. For example, during an uptrend, you may want to focus on buying growth stocks, while during a downtrend, you may want to focus on defensive stocks.

It's important to remember that while market cycles and trends can be helpful in making investment decisions, they are not foolproof. The stock market is inherently unpredictable, and past performance does not guarantee future results.

5. Conclusion

In this chapter, we've explored the concept of market cycles and trends and how they can impact your investments. By understanding these patterns, you can make more informed decisions and potentially profit from the stock market bull run. In the next chapter, we'll look at some of the hottest sectors to watch in the current market environment.

THREE

The stock market is composed of many sectors, each with its unique characteristics and trends. Understanding which sectors are hot and why they are hot is key to identifying potential investment opportunities.

In this chapter, we will explore some of the hottest sectors to watch and the opportunities and risks they present.

1. Defining Sectors

Before we dive into the hot sectors, let's first define what we mean by a sector. A sector is a group of companies that are involved in similar business activities. For example, the technology sector includes companies that develop and produce technology products and services.

The Global Industry Classification Standard (GICS) is the most widely used classification system for sectors. It divides the market into eleven sectors:

- Energy
- Materials
- Industrials
- Consumer Discretionary
- Consumer Staples
- Health Care
- Financials
- Information Technology
- Communication Services
- Utilities
- Real Estate

2. Hot Sectors to Watch

Now, let's explore some of the hottest sectors to watch.

1. Technology: The technology sector has been one of the hottest sectors for years. It includes companies that develop and produce technology products and services. Some of the biggest companies in the sector include

Apple, Microsoft, Amazon, and Facebook. The technology sector presents opportunities in areas such as artificial intelligence, cloud computing, and cybersecurity. However, it also presents risks such as volatility, regulation, and cybersecurity threats.

2. Healthcare: The healthcare sector includes companies that provide products and services related to healthcare. Some of the biggest companies in the sector include Johnson & Johnson, Pfizer, and Merck. The healthcare sector presents opportunities in areas such as biotechnology, pharmaceuticals, and medical devices. However, it also presents risks such as regulatory issues, drug pricing, and clinical trials.

3. Consumer Discretionary: The consumer discretionary sector includes companies that provide non-essential goods and services. Some of the biggest companies in the sector include Amazon, Home Depot, and Nike. The consumer discretionary sector presents opportunities in areas such as e-commerce, luxury goods, and leisure activities. However, it also presents risks such as changing consumer preferences, competition, and economic downturns.

4. Financials: The financial sector includes companies that provide financial services. Some of the biggest companies in the sector include JPMorgan Chase, Bank of America, and Wells Fargo. The financial sector presents opportunities in areas such as banking, insurance, and asset management. However, it also presents risks such as interest rate fluctuations, regulatory issues, and economic downturns.

3. Opportunities and Risks

While each sector presents unique opportunities, they also come with unique risks. It's important to carefully evaluate both the opportunities and the risks before making investment decisions.

When evaluating opportunities, consider factors such as:

- Market trends: Is the sector growing or shrinking?
- Competitive landscape: Who are the key players in the sector?
- Innovation: Is there a lot of innovation and potential for growth?
- Consumer demand: Are consumers interested in the products and services in the sector?
- Earnings growth: Are the companies in the sector experiencing strong earnings growth?

When evaluating risks, consider factors such as:

- Regulatory issues: Is the sector heavily regulated?
- Economic downturns: Is the sector vulnerable to economic downturns?

- Competition: Is there a lot of competition in the sector?
- Cybersecurity threats: Is the sector vulnerable to cybersecurity threats?
- Valuations: Are the companies in the sector overvalued?

4. Conclusion

Hot sectors can provide exciting investment opportunities, but they also come with unique risks. It's important to carefully evaluate both the opportunities and the risks before making investment decisions. By staying informed and up-to

FOUR

When it comes to evaluating stocks, there are two main approaches: fundamental analysis and technical analysis. Both can be useful for making informed investment decisions, and each has its own strengths and weaknesses. In this chapter, we'll explore both methods and discuss how to use them effectively.

1. Fundamental Analysis

Fundamental analysis involves evaluating a company's financial and economic fundamentals to determine its intrinsic value. This can include examining financial statements, such as the balance sheet, income statement, and cash flow statement, as well as analyzing key performance metrics like revenue growth, profit margins, and return on equity.

Some of the key indicators that investors look for in fundamental analysis include:

- Earnings per share (EPS)
- Price-to-earnings (P/E) ratio
- Price-to-book (P/B) ratio
- Dividend yield
- Debt-to-equity (D/E) ratio

By analyzing these factors, investors can gain a better understanding of a company's financial health and growth prospects. For example, a company with high revenue growth, low debt levels, and a reasonable P/E ratio may be a good investment opportunity.

However, fundamental analysis does have its limitations. It can be time-consuming and may not always capture short-term market fluctuations. Additionally, factors such as changes in management or unexpected events like a pandemic or economic recession can quickly impact a company's fundamentals.

2. Technical Analysis

Technical analysis, on the other hand, focuses on analyzing a stock's price and volume movements to identify patterns and trends. This can involve using technical indicators such as moving averages, relative strength index (RSI), and MACD (moving average convergence divergence).

By looking at historical price and volume data, technical analysts aim to identify trends and momentum in the market. For example, if a stock's price is trending higher and trading volume is increasing, this could indicate that there is strong buying pressure and the stock may continue to rise.

However, technical analysis also has its limitations. It can be subjective and may not always accurately predict future price movements. Additionally, technical analysis does not take into account a company's financial health or growth prospects.

3. Using Both Approaches

While fundamental and technical analysis are often viewed as separate approaches, many investors use both methods in combination to make investment decisions. This approach is sometimes called "fusion analysis."

By using both fundamental and technical analysis, investors can gain a more complete picture of a company's health and growth prospects, as well as the market trends and momentum that may impact its stock price.

However, it's important to remember that there is no foolproof method for predicting stock prices or market trends. Investing always involves some degree of risk, and it's important to do your own research and make informed decisions based on your own financial goals and risk tolerance.

4. Conclusion

Evaluating stocks using fundamental and technical analysis is an important part of making informed investment decisions. Both methods have their own strengths and weaknesses, and using both in combination can provide a more complete picture of a company's health and growth prospects.

As with any investment strategy, it's important to do your own research and make informed decisions based on your own financial goals and risk tolerance. By staying informed and taking a long-term approach to investing, you can increase your chances of success in the stock market bull run.

FIVE

Building a Diversified Portfolio: Asset Allocation and Risk Management

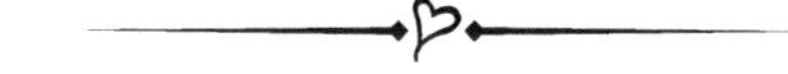

1. Introduction:

Investing in the stock market can be both exciting and daunting. It's important to build a diversified portfolio to manage risk and ensure long-term success. In this chapter, we'll discuss the principles of asset allocation and risk management to help you build a portfolio that's right for your investment goals and risk tolerance.

2. Understanding Asset Allocation:

Asset allocation is the process of dividing your investment portfolio across different asset classes, such as stocks, bonds, and cash. The goal is to achieve a balance between risk and reward that's appropriate for your individual needs and preferences.

For example, a young investor with a long investment horizon may want to allocate a higher percentage of their portfolio to stocks, which historically have higher returns but also higher volatility. On the other hand, an investor approaching retirement may want to allocate more of their portfolio to bonds, which offer lower returns but also lower risk.

3. Diversification:

Diversification is the practice of investing in a variety of assets within each asset class. The goal is to spread out risk and avoid putting all your eggs in one basket. For example, within the stock portion of your portfolio, you might invest in a mix of large-cap, mid-cap, and small-cap stocks, as well as stocks from different sectors and geographic regions.

Diversification can help reduce volatility and protect your portfolio from the ups and downs of individual stocks or sectors. However, it's important to note that diversification does not eliminate risk entirely.

4. Managing Risk:

Managing risk is an important part of building a successful investment portfolio. There are several strategies you can use to manage risk, including:

· Setting Realistic Expectations: It's important to have a realistic understanding of the potential risks and rewards of different investments. Don't expect to get rich quick, and don't invest more than you can afford to lose.

· Rebalancing: Over time, the value of your investments may shift, causing your portfolio to become unbalanced. Rebalancing involves selling assets that have done well and buying assets that have underperformed, in order to maintain your desired asset allocation.

· Dollar-Cost Averaging: Dollar-cost averaging involves investing a fixed amount of money at regular intervals, regardless of the market's ups and downs. This can help reduce the impact of market volatility on your portfolio.

· Using Stop-Loss Orders: A stop-loss order is an order to sell a stock if it drops below a certain price. This can help limit your losses in case of a sudden market downturn.

5. Conclusion:

Building a diversified portfolio and managing risk are essential components of successful investing in the stock market. By understanding the principles of asset allocation, diversification, and risk management, you can create a portfolio that's tailored to your individual needs and preferences. Remember to set realistic expectations, regularly rebalance your portfolio, use dollar-cost averaging, and consider using stop-loss orders to manage risk and protect your investments.

SIX

INVESTING IN EXCHANGE-TRADED FUNDS (ETFS)

Exchange-traded funds (ETFs) have become increasingly popular in recent years as a way for investors to gain exposure to a diversified portfolio of stocks or other assets in a cost-effective and convenient way. In this chapter, we'll explore what ETFs are, how they work, and the potential benefits and risks of investing in them.

1. What are ETFs?

ETFs are investment funds that trade on stock exchanges, just like individual stocks. Unlike traditional mutual funds, which are priced and traded once a day, ETFs can be bought and sold throughout the day at market prices. ETFs typically track a specific index, such as the S&P 500, or a specific sector or asset class, such as technology stocks or commodities.

2. How do ETFs work?

When you invest in an ETF, you're buying a share of a fund that holds a basket of underlying assets, such as stocks or bonds. The value of your ETF share is based on the value of the underlying assets. ETFs can be structured as either passive or active funds. Passive ETFs track a specific index and aim to replicate its performance, while active ETFs are managed by a professional fund manager and aim to outperform the market.

3. What are the potential benefits of investing in ETFs?

One of the biggest advantages of ETFs is their low cost. Because ETFs are passively managed and traded on exchanges, they generally have lower expense ratios than actively managed mutual funds. ETFs also offer instant diversification across a portfolio of assets, which can help reduce risk. Additionally, because ETFs are traded on exchanges, investors can buy and sell them throughout the day at market prices, providing flexibility and liquidity.

4. What are the potential risks of investing in ETFs?

Like any investment, ETFs carry some risks. One potential risk is tracking error - the possibility that the ETF's returns won't exactly match those of the underlying index it tracks. Additionally, some ETFs use leverage or other complex strategies, which can increase risk. Finally, because ETFs are traded on exchanges, they are subject to market volatility and may experience price fluctuations.

5. How can you invest in ETFs?

Investing in ETFs is relatively straightforward. You can buy and sell ETF shares through a brokerage account, just like you would with individual stocks. Many popular online brokerages offer commission-free ETF trading. Before investing in an ETF, it's important to research the underlying assets it holds, its expense ratio, and any other relevant information.

6. Conclusion

ETFs offer a convenient, low-cost way for investors to gain exposure to a diversified portfolio of assets. They can be a great option for investors looking to build a well-diversified portfolio while minimizing costs. However, like any investment, ETFs carry risks and should be approached with caution. By understanding how ETFs work and carefully researching any ETFs you're considering, you can make informed investment decisions that align with your financial goals.

SEVEN

Mutual funds are a popular investment option that offer several advantages to investors. In this chapter, we'll take a closer look at what mutual funds are, how they work, and the benefits and risks of investing in them.

1. What are Mutual Funds?

Mutual funds are investment vehicles that pool money from multiple investors to purchase a diversified portfolio of stocks, bonds, or other securities. Each investor owns a share of the mutual fund, which gives them exposure to a broad range of securities without having to buy and manage individual stocks or bonds.

2. How do Mutual Funds Work?

When you invest in a mutual fund, you are essentially handing over your money to a professional fund manager who invests it on your behalf. The fund manager uses the money to purchase a diversified portfolio of securities, with the goal of achieving the fund's investment objectives.

Mutual funds can be actively managed, where the fund manager makes regular investment decisions based on market conditions and other factors, or passively managed, where the fund simply tracks a specific index or benchmark.

3. Benefits of Investing in Mutual Funds

There are several benefits to investing in mutual funds:

· Diversification: By investing in a mutual fund, you can gain exposure to a wide range of securities, which helps to spread your risk and reduce the impact of individual stock or bond performance on your overall portfolio.

· Professional Management: Mutual funds are managed by professional fund managers who have expertise in investing and managing portfolios. This can be particularly beneficial if you don't have the time or expertise to manage your investments yourself.

· Convenience: Investing in a mutual fund is a convenient way to invest in the stock market, as you can simply buy and sell shares of the fund like you would any other security.

• Liquidity: Mutual funds are generally highly liquid, which means you can buy and sell shares easily and quickly.

4. Risks of Investing in Mutual Funds

Like any investment, mutual funds carry some risks:

• Market Risk: Mutual funds are subject to market risk, which means that the value of your investment can fluctuate based on market conditions.

• Fees: Mutual funds typically charge fees, such as management fees and expense ratios, which can eat into your returns.

• Underperformance: While mutual funds are managed by professionals, there is no guarantee that the fund will outperform the market or other investments.

• Lack of Control: When you invest in a mutual fund, you are essentially handing over control of your investments to the fund manager, which means you have less control over the individual securities in your portfolio.

5. Conclusion

Investing in mutual funds can be a convenient and effective way to gain exposure to the stock market and other securities. By pooling your money with other investors and having a professional fund manager make investment decisions on your behalf, you can benefit from diversification, professional management, and liquidity. However, mutual funds carry some risks, including market risk, fees, underperformance, and lack of control. Before investing in a mutual fund, it's important to carefully consider these risks and do your research to find a fund that aligns with your investment objectives and risk tolerance.

EIGHT

If you are interested in actively trading stocks, then you need to know the different trading strategies that are commonly used in the market. In this chapter, we will introduce you to three popular trading strategies: day trading, swing trading, and position trading.

1. Day Trading

Day trading involves buying and selling stocks within the same trading day. Day traders aim to profit from the fluctuations in the stock price throughout the day. They typically use technical analysis to identify short-term price movements and make quick trades to capitalize on them.

Day trading requires a lot of attention and discipline. Traders need to be constantly monitoring the market and have a well-defined strategy in place. It can be a high-risk, high-reward strategy, and it is not recommended for beginners.

2. Swing Trading

Swing trading is a strategy that involves holding stocks for a few days to a few weeks. Swing traders aim to profit from short-term price movements that occur within a larger trend. They use technical analysis to identify the entry and exit points for their trades.

Swing trading requires less attention than day trading, but still requires a disciplined approach. Swing traders need to be patient and wait for the right opportunities to enter and exit their trades. It can be a good strategy for those who cannot monitor the market constantly but still want to actively trade.

3. Position Trading

Position trading is a longer-term strategy that involves holding stocks for weeks to months or even years. Position traders aim to profit from the long-term trends in the market. They use fundamental analysis to identify undervalued or overvalued stocks and hold them for the long term.

Position trading requires even less attention than swing trading, but still requires a disciplined approach. Position traders need to be patient and have a long-term perspective. It can be a good strategy for those who want to invest in the stock market but do not want to actively trade.

4. Which Strategy is Right for You?

Choosing the right trading strategy depends on your goals, personality, and experience level. Day trading can be highly profitable but also highly stressful and requires a lot of attention. Swing trading can be a good compromise between day trading and position trading. Position trading can be less stressful but also requires a lot of patience and a long-term perspective.

Regardless of which strategy you choose, it is important to have a well-defined trading plan in place. This should include your entry and exit points, your risk management strategy, and your profit targets. You should also have a strict set of trading rules and follow them consistently.

5. Conclusion

Day trading, swing trading, and position trading are all popular trading strategies that can be used to profit from the stock market. Each strategy has its own advantages and disadvantages, and it is important to choose the one that best fits your goals and personality. Remember to always have a well-defined trading plan and stick to it consistently.

NINE

Options Trading: Strategies and Risks

Options trading is a popular strategy that allows investors to profit from the movements of stocks without actually owning them. Options are contracts that give the buyer the right, but not the obligation, to buy or sell a stock at a predetermined price within a certain time period. In this chapter, we will introduce you to the different options trading strategies and the risks associated with them.

1. Types of Options

There are two main types of options: call options and put options. A call option gives the buyer the right to buy a stock at a predetermined price, while a put option gives the buyer the right to sell a stock at a predetermined price.

Options Trading Strategies

• Covered Call Strategy

The covered call strategy involves owning the underlying stock and selling call options against it. This strategy can be used to generate additional income from the stock while limiting the potential downside risk.

• Protective Put Strategy

The protective put strategy involves buying a put option to protect against the downside risk of owning the underlying stock. This strategy can be used to limit potential losses while still allowing for potential gains.

• Straddle Strategy

The straddle strategy involves buying both a call option and a put option with the same strike price and expiration date. This strategy can be used to profit from significant price movements in either direction.

• Strangle Strategy

The strangle strategy is similar to the straddle strategy but involves buying a call option and a put option with different strike prices. This strategy can be used to profit from significant price movements in either direction while reducing the cost of the trade.

2. Risks of Options Trading

Options trading can be a high-risk strategy that is not suitable for all investors. The risks associated with options trading include:

• Time Decay Risk

Options contracts have an expiration date, and as the expiration date approaches, the value of the option may decrease.

• Volatility Risk

The value of options contracts is affected by the volatility of the underlying stock. High volatility can increase the value of options, while low volatility can decrease the value of options.

• Assignment Risk

When an option is exercised, the seller of the option must fulfill their obligation to buy or sell the underlying stock. This can result in unexpected losses for the seller.

3. Conclusion

Options trading can be a profitable strategy for experienced investors, but it is important to understand the risks associated with it. The different options trading strategies, such as the covered call strategy, protective put strategy, straddle strategy, and strangle strategy, offer different advantages and disadvantages. It is important to choose the strategy that best fits your goals and risk tolerance. Remember to always have a well-defined trading plan and stick to it consistently to mitigate the risks associated with options trading.

TEN

When it comes to trading in the stock market, emotions can play a big role in your success or failure. Fear and greed are two of the most common emotions that can lead traders to make irrational decisions. In this chapter, we will discuss how to overcome fear and greed and maintain a level-headed approach to trading.

1. Understanding Fear and Greed

Fear and greed are two emotions that are often linked in the world of trading. Fear can cause traders to hesitate, miss opportunities, or make impulsive decisions. Greed, on the other hand, can cause traders to take on too much risk or become overly confident in their trades.

It is important to understand that fear and greed are normal human emotions. However, when they start to influence your trading decisions, it can lead to poor performance and losses.

2. Overcoming Fear

To overcome fear in trading, it is important to have a solid trading plan and stick to it. This includes having clear entry and exit points, setting stop-loss orders, and using proper risk management techniques. By having a plan in place, you can avoid making impulsive decisions based on fear.

Another way to overcome fear is to practice. Start with a small trading account and gradually increase your position size as you become more comfortable with the process. This can help you build confidence in your abilities and reduce the impact of fear.

Finally, it can be helpful to surround yourself with a supportive trading community. This can provide you with encouragement and feedback, and help you stay on track when fear starts to creep in.

3. Overcoming Greed

To overcome greed, it is important to be disciplined in your trading approach. This includes sticking to your trading plan and avoiding impulsive decisions based on greed. It can also be helpful to set realistic profit targets and stick to them.

Another way to overcome greed is to focus on the long-term. Instead of trying to make a quick profit, focus on building a solid, sustainable trading strategy. This can help you avoid taking on too much risk in search of short-term gains.

Finally, it is important to practice gratitude and appreciate the progress you have made. Celebrate your successes and take time to reflect on what you have learned, rather than constantly chasing the next big win.

4. Conclusion

Overcoming fear and greed is essential to successful trading in the stock market. By understanding these emotions and how they can impact your decision-making, you can develop a disciplined approach to trading. Remember to have a solid trading plan in place, practice, surround yourself with a supportive community, be disciplined in your approach, focus on the long-term, and practice gratitude. By doing so, you can overcome fear and greed and become a successful trader.

ELEVEN

Tax-Efficient Investing Strategies

Investing in the stock market can be a great way to build wealth over time, but it is important to consider the impact of taxes on your investment returns. In this chapter, we will discuss tax-efficient investing strategies that can help you minimize your tax liability and maximize your after-tax returns.

1. Understand the Tax Implications of Your Investments

Before you start investing, it is important to understand the tax implications of your investments. Different types of investments are taxed differently, and it is important to know how your investments will be taxed. For example, dividends and capital gains are taxed differently, and some investments, such as municipal bonds, may be tax-free.

2. Utilize Tax-Advantaged Accounts

One of the best ways to minimize your tax liability is to invest in tax-advantaged accounts, such as 401(k) plans, individual retirement accounts (IRAs), and health savings accounts (HSAs). These accounts allow you to invest pre-tax dollars, which can reduce your taxable income and lower your tax bill. In addition, investment gains within these accounts are tax-deferred or tax-free, depending on the type of account.

3. Consider Tax-Loss Harvesting

Tax-loss harvesting is a strategy that involves selling losing investments to offset capital gains and reduce your tax liability. For example, if you have a stock that has decreased in value since you bought it, you can sell it and use the loss to offset capital gains from other investments. You can then reinvest the proceeds in a similar investment to maintain your overall portfolio allocation.

4. Use Tax-Efficient Investment Vehicles

Some investments are more tax-efficient than others. For example, exchange-traded funds (ETFs) and index funds tend to be more tax-efficient than actively managed mutual funds, which have higher turnover and generate more capital gains. In addition, investing in individual stocks can be more tax-efficient than investing in mutual funds or ETFs, as you have more control over when you realize capital gains.

5. Be Mindful of Tax Consequences When Rebalancing Your Portfolio

Rebalancing your portfolio involves adjusting your investments to maintain your desired asset allocation. However, it is important to be mindful of the tax consequences of your rebalancing decisions. For example, if you sell an investment that has appreciated significantly, you may generate a large capital gain that will increase your tax liability.

6. Conclusion

Taxes are an important consideration when investing in the stock market, and there are several strategies that can help you minimize your tax liability and maximize your after-tax returns. By understanding the tax implications of your investments, utilizing tax-advantaged accounts, considering tax-loss harvesting, using tax-efficient investment vehicles, and being mindful of tax consequences when rebalancing your portfolio, you can create a tax-efficient investment strategy that will help you reach your financial goals.

TWELVE

PASSIVE INVESTING: THE PROS AND CONS OF INDEX FUNDS

Index funds are a type of passive investment that seeks to track the performance of a particular stock market index, such as the S&P 500 or the NASDAQ. In this chapter, we will discuss the pros and cons of investing in index funds.

1. The Pros of Investing in Index Funds

• Low Cost: Index funds have lower expense ratios compared to actively managed mutual funds. This means that investors can save money on fees and expenses, allowing them to keep more of their investment returns.

• Diversification: Index funds invest in a broad range of stocks, providing investors with instant diversification. This reduces the risk of owning individual stocks and helps to spread risk across different sectors and industries.

• Consistent Performance: Index funds aim to track the performance of a particular index, which means that investors can expect consistent returns over the long term. While individual stocks may experience significant fluctuations, index funds provide more stable and predictable returns.

• Accessibility: Index funds are widely available and can be easily purchased through brokerage accounts or retirement plans. This makes them accessible to a wide range of investors.

2. The Cons of Investing in Index Funds

• Lack of Flexibility: Index funds are designed to track a particular index, which means that investors have limited control over the individual stocks that are included in the fund. This can be a disadvantage for investors who want to invest in specific stocks or sectors.

• Limited Upside Potential: While index funds provide consistent returns, they may not provide the same upside potential as individual stocks. This means that investors may miss out on significant gains if they only invest in index funds.

• Market Volatility: While index funds provide diversification and stable returns, they are still subject to market volatility. This means that investors may experience significant losses during market downturns.

• Passive Management: Index funds are managed passively, which means that they do not have a dedicated team of investment professionals actively managing the fund. While this reduces costs, it also means that there is no one actively making investment decisions on behalf of the fund.

3. Conclusion

Index funds are a popular type of passive investment that can provide low-cost diversification and consistent returns. While they have several advantages, such as low cost and broad diversification, they also have some disadvantages, such as lack of flexibility and limited upside potential. Ultimately, whether or not to invest in index funds depends on the individual investor's goals, risk tolerance, and investment strategy. It is important to carefully consider the pros and cons of index funds before making any investment decisions.

THIRTEEN

THE IMPACT OF ECONOMIC AND POLITICAL NEWS ON THE STOCK MARKET

The stock market is influenced by a variety of factors, including economic and political news. In this chapter, we will discuss how economic and political news can impact the stock market and how you can use this information to make informed investment decisions.

1. Economic News

Economic news can include reports on indicators such as gross domestic product (GDP), inflation, employment, and consumer spending. Positive economic news can lead to an increase in stock prices, while negative economic news can lead to a decrease.

For example, if there is a report indicating that the unemployment rate has decreased, this can lead to a boost in investor confidence and an increase in stock prices. On the other hand, if there is a report indicating that inflation has increased, this can lead to concerns about the economy overheating and a decrease in stock prices.

It is important to pay attention to economic news and understand how it can impact the stock market. However, it is also important to remember that economic news is just one factor among many that can influence the stock market.

2. Political News

Political news can also have a significant impact on the stock market. This can include news related to government policies, international relations, and geopolitical events. Positive political news can lead to an increase in stock prices, while negative political news can lead to a decrease.

For example, if a government announces a new policy that is seen as business-friendly, this can lead to an increase in investor confidence and an increase in stock prices. On the other hand, if there is a geopolitical event that creates uncertainty, such as a conflict between two countries, this can lead to a decrease in investor confidence and a decrease in stock prices.

It is important to pay attention to political news and understand how it can impact the stock market. However, it is also important to remember that political news can be unpredictable and difficult to forecast.

3. Using Economic and Political News in Your Investment Strategy

When making investment decisions, it can be helpful to take into account both economic and political news. This can help you make informed decisions and better understand the potential risks and opportunities in the market.

However, it is important to remember that economic and political news is just one factor among many that can impact the stock market. It is also important to have a well-diversified portfolio and a long-term perspective.

4. Conclusion

Economic and political news can have a significant impact on the stock market. Positive news can lead to an increase in stock prices, while negative news can lead to a decrease. It is important to pay attention to economic and political news and understand how it can impact the stock market. However, it is also important to remember that economic and political news is just one factor among many that can influence the stock market.

FOURTEEN

The stock market can be unpredictable and volatile, with sudden price swings and unexpected events. As an investor, it is important to be prepared for these market fluctuations and have a risk management strategy in place. In this chapter, we will explore some techniques to help you prepare for market volatility and protect your investments.

1. Diversification

One of the most basic risk management techniques is diversification. Diversification involves spreading your investments across different sectors, asset classes, and geographic regions. By diversifying your portfolio, you can reduce the impact of any one stock or market event on your overall portfolio.

2. Asset Allocation

Another important risk management technique is asset allocation. Asset allocation involves dividing your portfolio among different asset classes such as stocks, bonds, and cash. The goal is to balance your portfolio between riskier investments (such as stocks) and less risky investments (such as bonds) to achieve a desired level of risk and return.

3. Stop Loss Orders

Stop loss orders are another technique that can help you manage risk. A stop loss order is an instruction to sell a stock if it reaches a certain price. This can help you limit your losses if a stock starts to decline.

4. Hedging

Hedging is a technique used to reduce risk by taking an opposite position to your existing investment. For example, if you own a stock that you are concerned may decline in value, you could buy a put option to protect against the potential loss.

5. Margin of Safety

The margin of safety is another risk management technique that involves buying stocks at a discount to their intrinsic value. This provides a buffer against any potential losses and can help protect your investments during market downturns.

6. Conclusion

Market volatility is an inevitable part of investing in the stock market, and it is important to be prepared for it. By diversifying your portfolio, using asset allocation, implementing stop loss orders, hedging your investments, and buying stocks with a margin of safety, you can reduce your risk and protect your investments. Remember that risk management is an ongoing process and you should regularly review and adjust your strategy as needed.

FIFTEEN

Retirement planning is one of the most important financial goals for many people. To achieve a comfortable retirement, it is essential to have a long-term investing strategy that aligns with your goals and risk tolerance. In this chapter, we will discuss some long-term investing strategies that can help you achieve your retirement goals.

1. The Power of Compounding

One of the most important principles of long-term investing is the power of compounding. Compounding occurs when your investment earnings generate additional earnings over time. By reinvesting your earnings, your portfolio can grow exponentially over time.

To take advantage of compounding, it is important to start investing as early as possible. The earlier you start, the longer your investments have to compound. Even small amounts invested regularly over a long period of time can grow significantly with the power of compounding.

2. Diversification

Another key principle of long-term investing is diversification. Diversification means spreading your investments across different asset classes, industries, and geographies to reduce risk.

By diversifying your portfolio, you can potentially reduce your overall risk while still earning a reasonable return. This is because different assets may perform differently at different times, and diversification helps to smooth out the ups and downs in your portfolio.

3. Asset Allocation

Asset allocation is the process of dividing your investments among different asset classes such as stocks, bonds, and cash. Asset allocation is important because it can have a significant impact on your portfolio's risk and return.

The right asset allocation for you will depend on your goals, risk tolerance, and time horizon. A younger investor with a longer time horizon may be able to tolerate more risk and allocate a higher percentage of their portfolio to stocks. An older investor nearing retirement may want to allocate a higher percentage of their portfolio to bonds to reduce risk.

4. Passive Investing

Passive investing is a strategy that involves investing in low-cost index funds or exchange-traded funds (ETFs) that track a particular market index such as the S&P 500. Passive investing has become increasingly popular in recent years because it offers low fees, broad diversification, and the potential for market-like returns.

Passive investing can be a good long-term strategy for retirement planning because it eliminates the need for active stock picking and market timing. Instead, investors can focus on their asset allocation and let the market do the work of generating returns over the long term.

5. Conclusion

Long-term investing strategies are essential for retirement planning. By taking advantage of the power of compounding, diversification, and asset allocation, investors can potentially achieve their retirement goals while minimizing risk. Passive investing can be a good long-term strategy for retirement planning because it offers low fees, broad diversification, and the potential for market-like returns. It is important to start investing early and to have a well-defined investment plan that aligns with your goals and risk tolerance.

Notes

Printed by Libri Plureos GmbH in Hamburg,
Germany